Cold Reading For Business

by
Ian Rowland

Publication

Cold Reading For Business

by Ian Rowland

First edition

The idea of including a copyright notice in this, the age of the internet, is clearly an exercise in glorious futility. Nonetheless, if only out of nostalgic affection for a time when copyright actually meant something, here it is:

If you try to violate my copyright, I shall be forced to put a curse on you. This is not pleasant. I won't go into details but suffice it to say the curse involves pain, hardship and discomfort, plus projects and deals going horribly wrong, plus your flourishing career suddenly taking on a rather 'Hindenburg' trajectory. You have been warned.

Dedication

I dedicate this book to the countless people who have, over many years, helped me to shape and refine Cold Reading For Business. These include former work colleagues (back in the days when I had a proper job) and the students I've had the privilege of working with, either individually or in the classes I run. As the student learns from the teacher, so often the teacher learns from the student.

One of my 'Cold Reading For Business' classes in London. I get wonderful people attending these classes from all over the world and from many different business backgrounds.

A Quick Note About Me

I do three things so I have three websites.

www.ianrowland.com

This is about my work as a professional writer. In simple terms, I offer a complete 'start-to-finish' writing and publishing service. Technical writing, business, sales, marketing, creative... you name it, I've done it! I offer 35+ years experience across all media. In my career, I've helped more companies to sell a greater range of goods and services than anyone else you're likely to meet. I'm also a 'ghostwriter'! If you've got a book inside you, I can write it for you or guide you through the self-publishing process.

- - -

www.coldreadingsuccess.com

My website devoted to the art, science and joy of cold reading and what I call 'cold reading for business'. As well as providing free information and downloads, the site tells you about my three books on cold reading and the training I offer.

- - -

www.ianrowlandtraining.com

All about my talks and training for conferences, corporate groups and private clients. Main subjects include:

- The Practical Persuasion Method.
- Creative Problem-Solving.
- Leadership, Presence And Charisma.
- Unlock Your Mind.
- Be A Genius!
- Cold Reading For Business.

I also offer bespoke training packages to suit *your* needs. Clients to date include the FBI, Google, Coca-Cola, Unilever, the Ministry Of Defence, the British Olympics Team, the Crown Estate and many more. Full details on the site.

About My Cold Reading Books

Three Books For Three Reasons

I've written three books on different aspects of cold reading.

My first book, 'The Full Facts Book Of Cold Reading', describes how to talk to people so you sound psychic. In particular, it's about how you can make statements to a complete stranger that seem accurate. It's a *descriptive* book, not an instructional one. It doesn't *teach* a cold reading system and isn't meant to.

My second book, 'Super Psychic Readings', teaches my own system for giving what I call 'personal' readings. It enables you to give *any* kind of reading (tarot, astrology, graphology and so on) but there's very little to learn or memorise. (Just for the record, my readings are always free.)

This book, 'Cold Reading For Business', is about how to use cold reading techniques in *other* contexts that have nothing to do with the psychic industry. It's about establishing rapid rapport, building trust and being persuasive. I've taught CRFB to people from all walks of life and they seem to find it useful, particularly with regard to sales, 'people handling' and building or growing your own business.

Please Tell Your Friends

If you want to tell your friends about me and this book, which I hope you will, it helps me if you send them to my own website rather than to the lovely people at Amazon:

www.coldreadingsuccess.com

I *have* made this book available on Amazon (paperback only) because these days people think that if a book's not on Amazon it doesn't exist.

However, it's nicer for me if people order from my own website, where you will also find the Kindle version, extra information, free downloads, related products and discount deals not available elsewhere.

So, please direct your friends to me rather than to Amazon if at all possible.

Thank you!

Contents

Contact And Connection

The final CRFB benefit I want to mention is this: CRFB helps you to make good connections with people you meet. It is uniquely useful in situations where you aren't as well prepared, or as well briefed, as you might like to be in an ideal world.

There was a time, in the pre-internet era, when I was doing a lot of business-to-business (B2B) selling. I would sometimes visit ten different companies, from ten completely different industries, in the space of a few days. Even with the best will in the world, it was impossible for me to be comprehensively well-briefed on every prospect, every company and all their respective industries and markets.

One option was to be pleasantly honest about it: "I'm sorry, I have to admit I don't know a great deal about what you do. Why don't you tell me about it..." This worked fairly well. I could ask constructive questions, do some SPIN selling, build 'yes' sets, look for pain points and use other sales techniques I knew.

CRFB gave me another option: I could make *statements* about the client's work that seemed to be accurate. People responded positively to this because they felt I was well informed about their company or their market — which felt gratifying to them.

This helped me to make good connections with people and to have very productive meetings. It worked just as well as the other sales techniques I knew and often seemed to work better.

This is the one aspect of CRFB that some people object to on ethical grounds. They suggest it's unethical or manipulative, and that to give the impression you know more than you really do is no basis for a constructive working relationship. I am very familiar with these objections but I don't think they are valid. My only aim was to foster good connections and build strong rapport with people. CRFB helped me to do this in an age when researching prospects, and preparing for meetings, was far more difficult and time-consuming than it is today. Even now, when every company has a website and research is easier, I believe CRFB helps you to connect with people in a way that nothing else can match.

I've discussed the ethics of CRFB a hundred times and I respect that there are many shades of opinion. In the final analysis, all I can say is this: use CRFB if you want to and otherwise don't.

Who This Book Is For

This book is for you if:

- You want to learn how to apply the psychology of cold reading to business and professional situations.

- You are interested in successful communication and want a few extra tools for your 'communication toolbox'.

- You like to make good, strong connections with people and build rapport as rapidly and effectively as possible.

I first began teaching CRFB in 2008. Back then I used to call it 'Applied Cold Reading' or ACR. Same subject, different name. Since then, I've taught CRFB to countless people from all over the world and all walks of life: entrepreneurs, retailers, manufacturers, therapists, teachers, media professionals, people in the armed services and so on. At one of my public classes I even had a professional poker player turn up!

CRFB is useful and effective no matter what your work situation happens to be. However, I think it is *particularly* useful for people who are building or running their own business. It's often said that business is about people. If you're self-employed, you have to deal with a wide range of people: prospects, customers, suppliers, consultants, agencies, officials and so on. The more successfully you can communicate with people, the better.

My Background

I'm including this information only because it's relevant to the *credibility* of the information in this book.

By trade, I'm a freelance writer. My first job was in creative media and marketing, back in the eighties when corporate video seemed new and exciting. It wasn't the greatest job in the world but it did offer plenty of variety. I wrote and produced creative material for a very broad range of companies: service, retail and manufacturing; at home and abroad; from small local businesses to large multinationals.

Some of the projects I worked on concerned training and education. However, the majority fell into the 'sales and promotion' category. I helped more companies to sell more products and services than you can possibly imagine: adhesives, cheese, engineering, lingerie, pet food, sugar beet, headache tablets, bicycles, weed killer, insurance, pallet wrappers, cranes, shoes, water pipes, double-glazing and tank turrets (seriously).

This work spanned print, audio, video and live events. No two days were ever the same. Sometimes I was out on the road selling my company's services. Other times I was writing, making a video, having script meetings, briefing other 'creatives' or collapsing in an exhausted heap.

Via several happy flukes and accidents, I ended up as what's called a 'technical author' in the software trade. In accordance with The Peter Principle, I somehow ended up as the UK Head of Sales & Marketing for an international internet technologies company. This was great fun because we were a *relatively* small firm pitching for large accounts against industry giants — and we often won!

Finally, I took the plunge and decided to work for myself, which I've now done for over 20 years. In the process, I've made myself phenomenally wealthy with homes on three continents, a luxury yacht and my own private jet. No, that's not true. I'm not even remotely wealthy. But I'm doing all right, love my work and get to meet a lot of great people.

Here's the point: I've done a lot of selling across the board. I have senior management experience and I've run my own successful business for more than two decades. When I say CRFB works, *I'm speaking from experience.* And plenty of it.

More importantly, CRFB will work for you as well.

A personal, one-to-one training session in London.

Interlude

One of the courses I teach is about practical persuasion skills. Whenever people enquire about it, an interesting situation arises. If I successfully persuade the client to go ahead and hire me, this suggests I know what I'm talking about. On the other hand if I *fail* to do so, this suggests I'm *not* very persuasive, so the course would have been a waste of time so they were right not to hire me. Either of the two options instantly validates itself, which I find quite pleasing.

One such enquiry came from the wonderful people at Coca-Cola European Partners who, I'm delighted to say, eventually made me an offer: would I like to present my course to some of their senior management over in Lisbon? It was clearly a tough decision. Would I like to work for the world's most recognised brand in one of Europe's most beautiful cities? Eventually, after evaluating all the pros and pros, I said yes.

I actually presented my course at the company's manufacturing plant on the outskirts of the city: a vast palace of breathtaking industrial genius wherein water is consecrated into the world's most popular drink with brain-dazzling efficiency. It was a wonderfully happy gig and also educational. I learned there's one thing you can do in Lisbon that you can't do in any other European capital city. Want to know the answer? It's on the website, in the Vault!

Role

Consider the meeting you are about to have. Think about how you want to define your role within the meeting, in the sense of *how you want to be perceived by the OP*.

Every time you meet someone, you are playing a role whether you realise it or not — just like an actor playing a part in a play or a film. Whatever your chosen role happens to be, it will have *implications* about your knowledge, expertise, background, attitude and character. Think about these implications and ask yourself if you look and sound right.

Do you behave in a way that's consistent with your role and the implications that go with it? If your role is 'very well informed consultant', make sure you look, sound and act like one. Likewise if your role is 'hard-working, creative graphic designer' or 'software geek full of bright ideas and smart solutions'.

Present a clear role and follow it through. The OP needs to know who you are, what you are and what you claim (this can be implicit or explicit). The OP can't have a clear idea of your role unless you do.

Always strive to fit your chosen role and bring it to life. Imagine watching an actor playing a cowboy. If he wore a pinstripe suit and had a basketball, you wouldn't think he was doing a very good job. Yet many people make similar mistakes when they go into meetings. They don't look or sound right and haven't prepared appropriately.

When I teach CRFB, I encourage my students to define their Role in 'superhero' terms. For example, instead of, 'I am a well qualified financial consultant,' say, 'I am literally the greatest financial genius you could ever meet.'

My view is that if you're going to choose a Role for yourself, you may as well 'think big' and have fun with it. One of my students suggested that superhero descriptions are also a form of positive reinforcement that could help your confidence. By all means see superhero descriptions in this light if you want, but I recommend them just because they're fun.

CRFB involves four steps: Define, Empathise, State, Advance.

We're looking at Step 1, 'Define'. This involves defining three elements of the meeting you are going to have. The first was the context (who / where / how) and the second was your Role (superhero description).

The third is your Intention.

Intention

You define your Intention in terms of what you want the OP to *feel, think* or *believe* as a result of the call or meeting. You can express it very simply like this:

"I want the OP to feel / think / believe [whatever it is]."

The 'feel / think / believe' part is a *choice*. You pick *one* of the three options.

If the appeal you want to make is primarily *emotional*, and to do with feelings rather than facts, use 'feel'.

If the appeal you want to make is primarily logical and *rational*, based on facts and figures, use 'think'.

If the appeal you want to make is primarily to do with 'buy in' to a particular belief system, use 'believe'.

'Feel' is the first and default option because feelings usually matter more than anything else. As every psychologist will tell you, people *can* behave rationally when they have to, but they live their lives through their *emotional* circuits and base most of their views and decisions on emotional factors.

Your intention (as defined here) is not the same as the *overall* goal for your meeting. You may be visiting the OP hoping she'll place an order for your product. However, your FTB Intention might be:

"I want the OP to *feel* she can trust me to provide the best service."

Other typical FTB Intentions might sound like this:

"I want the OP to *think* that I'm likely to have the best solutions to his technical problems."

"I want the OP to *believe* that hypnotherapy is well accredited and very likely to help her."

In these examples, you could substitute 'my company' for 'me', though I think it's usually better to express your intention in personal terms.

As with defining your context and role, the point of defining your intention is that it helps you to prepare for meetings as successfully as possible. Just the fact that you're giving some thought to your intention can spur good

Tip #1:Health, Wealth, Spirit

If you struggle to even start empathising with the OP's situation, you can at least focus on three aspects of her life: health, wealth and spirit. In my CRFB class, we call these an 'empathy starter pack'!

When you think about the OP, in what way might her work affect her physical, mental and emotional *health*? Is she likely to suffer from fatigue, stress, strain, aches, anxiety or something else?

Next, think about *wealth*. Is she likely to be earning good money and enjoying a nice standard of living, or struggling to make ends meet? Also, think about other forms of wealth. Is she likely to find satisfaction and fulfilment in her work? Does her job give her an opportunity to *demonstrate* her aptitudes, creativity and business acumen, or is it more likely to *stifle* them? Does she feel appreciated or taken for granted?

Finally, think about her *spirit*. This isn't an easy word to define, but in loose terms I'm referring to the OP's character and the sort of 'energy' she gives off. Do you get the feeling she starts every day feeling bright, cheery and optimistic, or empty and despondent? Does you get the sense she's living life to the full or barely keeping the car on the road? Does she smile more than she frowns or vice-versa?

Just by considering these three aspects of someone's life, you can start to empathise with her situation and to see how the world looks from her point of view.

Empathising with people and their problems is a skill and, as such, the only way to develop proficiency is to practise, regularly and often, so you build up your experience. Fortunately, this is easy to do. You see hundreds of people all around you every day: the young woman on her laptop in the coffee shop, the doorman of the fancy hotel, the woman on the bus with two kids and a ton of shopping, the teenage lovers on the park bench. Think about all these people and try to empathise with their situation (without staring or making anyone feel uncomfortable).

Of course, this type of empathy is necessarily *speculative*. You will rarely, if ever, get the chance to check with people and learn whether your guesses about their problems are correct or not. However, it's all good practice. What's more, when you use the CRFB process, it doesn't matter if your speculations turn out to be wrong — for reasons we'll get to later.

Empathy tip #1 was Health, Wealth, Spirit — the empathy 'starter pack'. Let's look at tip #2.

Tip #2: Mirror Me

Here's a simple tip you might find useful when trying to empathise with people: think about negative aspects of your *own* life and ask yourself whether any of them are likely to affect the OP as well.

I'm sure you can think of several frustrations, annoyances and irritations that render your life slightly less than perfect. Maybe you have to work with one or two people you don't get on with very well. Maybe some of your company's systems and processes strike you as annoyingly out of date or tedious. Whatever your own pains and problems happen to be, ask yourself whether the OP is also likely to have to deal with them.

In some cases, the answer will be 'almost certainly yes' or 'almost certainly no'. Most of them time you won't feel it's quite such an easy call, but at least you will be practising your ability to empathise with people and their problems.

Tip #3: Ten Sec Check

If you want to improve your ability to empathise with people, another good idea to try is the Ten Sec Check.

Here's how it works. You're trying to empathise with someone, speculating about her problems, challenges and difficulties. Let's assume you have come up with one or two possibilities.

At this point, take ten seconds to check if there's a better answer waiting to be found. Ask your mind to go beyond your first thoughts and drill down to something deeper and less obvious. Tell yourself there's gold waiting to be discovered if you just stretch your mental and emotional muscles a little further and try to come up with a more subtle point.

Here's a curious example from my own working life. I used to work as a freelance technical writer. This meant, for example, being assigned to a company for three months to create all the documentation for their new online service. All the contracts were of the high pressure, fast turnaround, tight deadline variety. What did I most dislike about the job: the constant pressure, the hours spent travelling, unrealistic client demands?

Actually, the most disappointing aspect of the job was *not getting the satisfaction of finishing a project*. A surprising number of software projects are started but never get finished for all sorts of reasons (such as a change of management). So I often worked hard on a project, only to discover they had decided not to complete it. I found this rather annoying — and it also meant I had fewer completed projects on my CV or resumé.

There's only one service provider so I have no choice who I use. Some downloads take over an hour, and frequently require several attempts. When I need to upload a large file, which I often do, I can't do any other internet-related work for fear of causing the upload to fail."

(2) The weather.

"As I work from home, you wouldn't think I'd be much affected by the weather. But in fact it's a constant worry. I am totally dependent on the utility companies for my electricity, phone and internet. In each case, there's only one provider. The infrastructure is unreliable but, as far as the companies are concerned, not worth improving. So every year things just get worse. Even a bit of rain or snow can knock out one or more services for hours. Sometimes, I don't know if or when I'll have power or internet access again. Could be in a hour, could be days."

- - -

I hope you enjoyed trying these exercises. It doesn't matter whether you came up with answers that matched their reports (although you can congratulate yourself if you did!). All that matters is that you tried.

If you'd want to improve your ability to empathise with people, here's an idea. Whenever you get the chance to talk to a stranger, politely ask them to share one thing they really like about their job (that an outsider would be unlikely to guess) and one thing they really hate about it (ditto). I've been doing this for years! You'll have some fascinating conversations and, at the same time, improve your ability to empathise with people.

Progress Review

CRFB involves four main steps: Define, Empathise, State, Advance.

We have already looked at Step 1, 'Define'.

In this section, we looked at Step 2, 'Empathise'. We looked at three tips that can help you to empathise with people:

- Health, Wealth, Spirit.

- Mirror Me.

- The Ten Sec Check.

Now we can look at Step 3, 'State'.

Interlude

Everything I know about sport could fit on the tip of a golf bat. My life is sadly, utterly devoid of sporting knowledge or interest. Despite this lamentable ignorance, I do sometimes get to work with sports organisations, including the British Olympics team. I'm told that good rapport and communication skills, for example between coach and athlete, are vital for achieving peak performance.

On one such occasion, I was invited to give a keynote speech at the STTAR Summit (Science, Training, Technology, Analytics and Rehabilitation) held at the Philadelphia 76ers' vast training complex. This proved to be a hugely enjoyable gig: luxurious hotel, delightful private dinner for all the speakers (where I performed a small show, naturally) and smart, efficient organisation every step of the way.

The 'goody' bag that I and all the speakers received was absurdly generous. Among other neat gifts, it contained a personalised 76ers shirt and a replica of the Liberty Bell (not life-size). I did offer to take the *real* Liberty Bell back home with me to London, where it came from, to get it fixed. My offer was politely, yet firmly, declined.

Heads You Win, Tails You Don't Lose

"Communication is the breath or death of any relationship."

— Rasheed Ogunlaru

Define	Context	(Who / Where / How)
	Role	(Superhero)
	Intention	(Feel / Think / Believe)
Empathise	H / W / S	
	Mirror Me	
	Ten Sec Check	
State	Subject	
	Statement	(50/50)
	Revision	(FASTMAM)
Advance		

Step 3: State

Step 3 of the CRFB process is about making a statement to the OP.

This involves what we call a *triplet*. A triplet consists of three elements:

- Subject.

- Statement.

- Revision.

I'll explain what I mean by each of these terms.

Subject

In CRFB, a subject is what you are going to make a statement *about*. It is *usually* a problem or negative emotion identified by empathising with the OP.

There are exceptions. Sometimes, you might choose a subject that refers to *positive* aspects of the OP's job rather than negative ones. For example, you might comment on her company's recent growth or successful product launch. However, problems and negative feelings are *usually* more fertile territory.

Choosing subjects is straightforward:

- Empathise with the OP, as discussed in Step 2.

- By doing this, identify negative feelings and emotions she is likely to experience in her working day.

- Choose one of these feelings (whichever you are most confident about).

- Express it as a short heading (ideally just one word but never more than two or three). This is your Subject.

Revision

In CRFB, the third part of a triplet is a revision.

A revision is defined as: 'what you say if you get a negative reply'. It's a way to turn an apparently incorrect statement into one that is correct after all.

As we have seen, CRFB involves offering statements that stand a roughly 50% chance of being true. If the OP responds positively to your statement, it's a 'hit' and you get the credit for being astute, smart, perceptive and well informed. But what if the OP responds negatively? This isn't a problem. You just use a revision so that your statement seems to be correct after all. Heads you win, tails you don't lose.

Let's see how these revisions work. There are seven in all. In each case I'll give you the revision's basic pattern followed by two examples of how it sounds: one from the psychic industry and one from the business world.

The business examples I provide here necessarily have to be rather generalised in nature and might not resonate with you. In real life, of course, you would be discussing specific issues and details. In the case of each revision, look at the underlying pattern and think how you might use it in *your* typical business conversations.

The seven revisions we're going to look at are:

- Focus.

- Awareness.

- Subjective.

- Time.

- Metaphor.

- Apply.

- Measurement.

The first letters spell 'FASTMAM', which may help you to remember them.

Focus

This revision *only* applies to statements that contain two or more ideas.

Pattern: If the OP responds positively to *one* idea you mentioned (out of two or more), focus on that *as if it was the only thing you mentioned*.

You do *not* explain or justify this. You simply focus on the one point that seems to resonate with the OP and talk about it *as if this was the only thing you mentioned*.

Psychic Example

> "I'm sensing a connection with a large country overseas, possibly beginning with 'A', and I'm being given a name that could be Mike or Michael or something like that, possibly a family or work connection."

Notice that this 'scattershot' statement contains numerous different ideas: large country, letter 'A', Michael or similar, family or work connection.

> *Client: "I have a cousin called Mike. Could that be what you mean?"*

> "Good, Mike, yes, that's what was coming through, and what I want to say to you about Mike is that..."

The psychic carries on as if the name 'Mike' was all she ever mentioned.

Business Example

> "I know it's been quite a difficult time in your industry — a lot of fresh competition, plus new security regulations and some shifts in consumer spending patterns not to mention the impact of new technology. It must be pretty exhausting!"

> *OP: "Well, we certainly have our work cut out keeping up with the latest technology, that's true."*

> "Exactly. The technology is evolving all the time and it's hard to keep track. This is one of the areas where I think we can really help, which is why I wanted to meet."

You carry on as if 'keeping up with technology' was the only issue you mentioned.

Aware

Pattern: My statement is correct, but maybe you're not aware of all the facts (which is perfectly okay).

Psychic Example

"This friend of yours [that we've been talking about] has a legal issue on her mind, something that's been worrying her quite a lot."

Client: "I don't think so. No. There's nothing like that."

"Ah, maybe she hasn't mentioned it to you. She knows you're a very caring person and if she told you about this, you'd want to help and you'd worry about it too. She may not want to trouble you about it so that's why she hasn't mentioned it."

Business Example

"I expect another major headache for you is compliance with the new regulations that are being introduced this year."

OP: "No, not really. I don't think that's much of a problem for us."

"Well, of course, that's rather low-level, detailed stuff that doesn't necessarily concern you. Yours is a much more high-level, strategic role so you probably wouldn't have much to do with that."

The vital thing about the Aware revision is that you must never make the OP feel insulted or criticised. You must never imply that the OP isn't aware of something he or she *should* be aware of, or that they haven't been paying attention to important details.

Always make it clear that if the OP isn't aware of something, it's probably for a very good reason that involves an element of flattery: they are too important to be bothered with such small details or they have greater responsibilities on their mind.

You can make the flattery flow in the opposite direction so it favours the 'lower ranks'. You can say the subject you've mentioned is the kind of thing the 'suits' waste their time idly chatting about in the board room sipping coffee, while the OP is being productive and actually getting some work done!

Subjective

This revision only applies to statements that contain a positive value judgment, such as saying something is going well or is good news.

Pattern: You declare that something is good news. The OP disagrees. You say you can understand how she feels, but it is good news if you look at it a different way (or from someone else's point of view).

Psychic Example

"There are signs here of very positive indications to do with your work and career and you have probably had some good news in that regard."

Client: "Er, no, not really. I lost my job two weeks ago."

"Well, I can understand you might feel that's rather bad news, of course! But the tarot often suggests a long-term view or a different way of interpreting life's events. For example, you'll find that this is a great opportunity to take stock and get a clearer picture about what you really want to do. You'll also explore opportunities that you wouldn't have tried if you were still doing the old job, and you'll end up in a better place. So, it is actually good news, although it might not feel like it at the moment."

Business Example

"I understand this has been a period of growth and expansion for your company."

OP: "No, not really. As a matter of fact we've had to close one branch and let a few people go."

"Well, I can understand that might not seem very positive at the moment. But 'growth' can take many forms. I'd say the fact that you've been able to take those difficult decisions — during what is, by any standards, a very tough market — means you're one of the leaner, fitter companies that will be well poised to exploit the better trading conditions when they come along. You prune the tree now but it yields more fruit later. That's really what I was getting at."

When we looked at choosing subjects for triplets, I said that the subject is *usually* but not *always* based on negative feelings (that you identified by empathising with the OP). It *is* possible to use subjects that refer to positive things, such as good news or welcome developments. Obviously, the Subjective revision will only arise in conjunction with positive statements.

It's usually easy to spot the Subjective revision. It tends to involve phrases like these:

> "I can understand it might look/feel bad now, but in fact..."

> "Well, I can understand you might not feel it's all that great. But you know, if you look at it from [some other angle] it *is* actually good news and that's what I was getting at."

In a business context, this revision often involves the notion of 'stakeholders'. If a company makes ten people redundant, is this good news or bad? Well, it depends entirely on which point of view you choose. Assuming those ten people didn't want to lose their jobs, it's bad news from their perspective. What about the other workers who kept their jobs? If they liked the people who were fired, bad news. If they couldn't stand them, and regarded them as 'slackers' anyway, then it's good news.

If you're the manager who was responsible for firing these people, you might not have enjoyed having to do it (bad news) but you will shine in the eyes of your boss and shown that you can take the tough decisions, which augurs well for your future (good news).

If you're one of this company's suppliers, and they buy lots of widgets from you every year, you neither know nor care how many people they've laid off. You just want them to stay in business so they'll continue to buy lots of stuff from you. If they've taken some decisions that enable them to stay in business, it's good news for you.

Hence you can usually make a case for almost anything being 'good', so long as you just see it from the correct point of view.

Never use the Subjective revision to go in the other direction and argue that something is *bad* news. Always start with a positive statement and, if the OP has doubts or disagrees, use this revision to show that whatever you mentioned *is* good news provided you look at it the right way.

Time

Pattern: If what I say isn't true now, it *was* at some point in the past *or* it *will be* at some point in the future.

You have to choose whether you shift to the past or future tense. It's one or the other, not both. Which do you choose? It always depends on the situation. You just choose whichever timeframe is safest, or seems most likely to work, or seems to make the most sense.

This is one of the most versatile and reliable of all revisions and can be applied to almost any statement.

Psychic Example

"This friend [that we have been talking about in the reading] has long hair, doesn't she?"

Client: "No. She actually wears her hair very short."

"Ah... I see where I was getting a bit confused. She wore her hair much longer when she was younger. She may have short hair now for practical reasons or whatever, but I can sense that she loved her long hair when she was a little girl and deep down she wishes she could still wear her hair like that."

Business Example

"I know that one headache you've got at the moment is the new regulation on date security and all the compliance details that go with it."

OP: "No. Not really. It's not an issue for us."

"Well, no, not right *now* it isn't. I understand that. What I mean is that, looking ahead, the picture's always changing and there will come a time when you have to address it. Which is actually one good reason for us to be talking now, while there's plenty of time to plan ahead."

Metaphor

Pattern: The statement may not be correct if taken literally, but you meant it in a metaphorical way.

Any statement can be understood literally or in several non-literal ways (metaphorically, figuratively, poetically and so on). When you shift to *any* non-literal meaning, this the Metaphor revision. The usual phrasing is 'When I said [x], what I actually meant was [a different way of interpreting x]."

Psychic Example

"The cards suggest you're someone who likes to travel a lot."

Client: "No, not really. I don't like airports and passports and all that fuss. I'm happy when I'm at home."

"Well, when I say 'travel' I don't necessarily mean in the literal sense of going all over the world. What I really meant was, for example, you like going a long way in your imagination — you're very creative. Also, you've 'come a long way' in the sense that you're quite a different person now than in your early adult years. You might say you've travelled a long way spiritually."

Business Example

"I understand this has been a period of expansion for you in terms of bringing new products to the market, developing new lines and so on. I expect it's involved quite a lot of pressure."

OP: "Not really. We have our core products and we pretty much just stick to those."

"Oh, sure, and it's an excellent policy. When I said expansion I didn't necessarily mean *actually* developing new products. That was just an example. I meant you're constantly exploring new ways of serving your market, engaging with customers, building your brand and things like that. Expanding your horizons, if you like."

The Metaphor revision also covers any shift from *actuality* to *aspiration*. For example, you might shift from "You've been gaining a lot of market share," to, "Well, I meant you would *like* to...," or "I hear that you're *planning* to...".

Apply

Pattern: If what I said doesn't apply to you, maybe it applies to others around you.

In the psychic industry, 'others around you' generally refers to the client's spouse, partner, relatives, neighbours or work colleagues.

In the business world, 'others around you' could refer either to people the OP works with, or to other companies in the same market or same industry.

In most cases, it helps if you can think of a reason why this difference between the OP and other people / companies is a *good* thing.

Psychic Example

"You have a legal matter that's been preying on your mind for some time. There could be a significant sum of money involved."

Client: "No, not really. Nothing I can think of."

"Mm, that's interesting because it's something I'm picking up on quite clearly. If this doesn't mean anything to you then maybe it's a friend or neighbour — but someone quite close to you had something like this on their mind. They might come asking for your help, so you may want to look out for that."

Business Example

"I know that one of the problems you're currently dealing with is outsourcing less and bringing more production back in-house."

OP: "That's not an issue for us. We're pretty happy with the balance between what we manufacture here and what we outsource."

"Sure, and I'm very glad to hear that. It means you've already figured out how to get the balance right. I only mentioned it because it's a problem a lot of companies I see are still struggling with. The fact that you *don't* have this problem is a good sign, and in fact it suggests you're one of the companies we can partner with most successfully."

Measurement

This revision only applies to statements that involve units of measurement, whether stated or implied. Hence you would normally only use it if your statement made reference to size, scale, scope, duration, numbers or statistics.

Pattern: The statement is right if you change *how* something is measured.

Psychic Example

"And this friend [that has come up in the reading] is a little older than you, isn't she?"

Client: "No, actually, she's a little younger."

"Yes, she may be younger in terms of her actual age, but don't you find she sometimes shows a maturity beyond her years? Also, I sense that some of her interests and tastes, for example in music, would usually be associated with someone a little older than her."

In this example, the psychic has shifted from assessing 'age' in the usual way (years since birth) to other ways such as emotional maturity or tastes and preferences. This is a Measurement revision but you could also think of it, at least in part, as a Metaphor revision.

Business Example

"As I understand it, your company has grown quite a bit in recent years."

OP: "No, not really. I'd say we're still a fairly small company, by industry standards."

"Oh, sure, I wasn't implying you've taken on hundreds more staff or anything. But I mean you've grown a lot in terms of your goals, ambitions, your plans to diversify, the way you've built your brand and so on."

Any reference to a company having 'grown' usually provides an opportunity to use the Measurement revision, or a blend of Measurement and Metaphor. To say a company has 'grown' *normally* refers to its scale (how many offices and branches it has), number of employees or revenue/profits. However, you could also be referring to the scope of the company's ambitions and goals, its presence in the market, its products and lines, its potential or its fitness to respond to market conditions or any one of several other factors. In business terms, 'growth' is a very fluid and versatile concept.

The Measurement revision is highly versatile, especially when you remember that almost all measurements are relative. Is my hand large? Compared with the moon, no, but compared with a pin, yes. Whenever you offer a statement that involves measurement, you can often make it correct by greatly exaggerating the opposite meaning. A couple of examples will show you what I mean.

"And last year you significantly improved your market share, didn't you?"

"No, not really. I think we're only up about 1.5% on last year."

"Well, that's kind of what I meant. I mean, I see a lot of companies who have either seen their share go down four or five points, maybe even more, or who are racing flat out just to stand still. Trust me, with the market the way it is, a lot of the players in your market would consider any gains at all pretty impressive, and 1.5% is a real success story."

You can see the pattern. When you wildly exaggerating the opposite idea, you can make your statement seem more plausible. I can take exactly the same example and make it flow the other way:

"And last year, you didn't really see much improvement in your market share, did you?"

"Actually, I think we did very well. We're up about 1.5% on last year."

"Well, that's kind of what I meant. I mean, it's certainly an achievement to be proud of and I wasn't implying otherwise. But in an ideal world you'd like to be seeing figures like 3, 4 or even 5% wouldn't you? And given all the hard work that you and everyone else have put in, that sort of increase would feel a lot more satisfying, wouldn't it?"

Same facts, different way of talking about them. This is why the Measurement revision is so versatile.

Statements and Revisions

It should now be clear how statements and revisions work together. Each time you devise a 50/50 statement, you *also* think ahead and plan which revision you could use if you get a negative response. In business situations, you will probably use Apply, Time and Metaphor most often. However, it's nice to have the other four should you need them.

Once you have gained a little experience with CRFB, you'll find you don't even need to plan ahead in this way. You'll be able to improvise on the spur of the moment. So long as you understand how each revision works, you'll find you can more or less instantly select the one you need whenever you need it. A little practice is all it takes.

Blending Revisions

You normally only need one revision at a time. However, it is sometimes appropriate to blend two revisions. We have already seen examples of revisions that blend Measurement and Metaphor. Another option that's often quite useful is to blend Time with Aware, like this:

> "Of course there's no reason why you would be dealing with any of this [subject I mentioned] *now*. It's probably not important enough for you to be involved at this stage. I just meant that there will probably come a point where people will want your input, given your experience."

You can see how this blends the Time revision (in this case shifting from the present to the future) with the Aware revision which, as usual, includes a neat garnish of flattery.

Not *every* conceivable pair of revisions go together well. I doubt one would ever find Focus teamed up with Subjective. Nonetheless, you may like to go through the practical exercise of considering various combination of revisions and asking yourself how they might sound and when you might use them.

Positive And Negative Responses

When you make an CRFB statement, there are (in simple terms) two possible responses: positive or negative. You can feel perfectly relaxed and confident either way. Positive responses count as a 'hit' and negative ones aren't a problem. Let's look at how you would handle either type of response.

Basically Positive. If you make a statement and the OP accepts it or agrees with it, all is well. You have demonstrated empathy and managed to come across as well informed and perceptive — achieving all the things I listed under the Tarot Comparison at the start of this book. This positive mood of agreement is a good platform on which to build the rest of your conversation or meeting.

In addition, you can sometimes use a positive response to *validate* your Role. For example, suppose you want the OP to feel you're well informed about current problems in her industry. You might say something like this:

"I expect another complication for you right now is the need to update the CRM system to handle currency conversions automatically."

"Tell me about it! Yes, that's certainly taking up quite a bit of our IT department's time."

"Yes, I felt that had to be the case, based on my research."

You are explaining the *reason* (your hypothetical 'research') for your apparently correct statement. This validates your Role. You wouldn't want to use this technique with *every* statement that gets a positive response. Endless repetition would dull its effectiveness. However, using it once or twice in a meeting or discussion can be a nice touch.

Basically Negative. If you get a negative response, you use one of the seven revisions we've just looked at, either individually or in combination.

It's *easy* to remember these two possibilities:

Positive > use for validation (occasionally).

Negative > use a revision.

With respect to negative responses, the only other thing you need to know about is the FIN Principle, which is what we'll look at next.

The Way Forward

"People will be more interested in you when you are interested in them. If you want to impress, talk to them about . . . them."

— Susan C. Young

Define	Context	(Who / Where / How)
	Role	(Superhero)
	Intention	(Feel / Think / Believe)
Empathise	H / W / S	
	Mirror Me	
	Ten Sec Check	
State	Subject	
	Statement	(50/50)
	Revision	(FASTMAM)
Advance		

Step 4: Advance

Step 4 of the CRFB process is 'Advance'.

This simply means linking the statement you made (and revision if necessary) to the agenda for the meeting or conversation. The point is to carry the conversation forward, to 'advance' it, in a purposeful way. It tends to involve phrases like this:

> "...and that's exactly why I felt it would be a good idea for us to talk today."

> "...which is really why I felt my company is in a perfect position to help you."

> "...so, all in all, I think you can see why we'd be able to help with what you're trying to achieve."

This is an important final part of the CRFB process. It's all very well knowing how to empathise with the OP, devise a statement and use a revision. However, there's no point in doing this if you just leave the conversation hanging in the air! It would be like getting in a car that's not going anywhere.

Having made your statement, and handled the positive or negative response appropriately, *advance* the conversation by linking what you said to your own agenda or to the purpose of the meeting. There are any number of ways to do this.

If you have just referred to a problem, it would be natural to discuss how you/your company can help the OP to address that problem and what type of solution you would suggest.

Conversely, if you have just referred to some good news or positive developments, you might want to suggest how you can make a good situation even better, help the OP to maximise the benefits or make sure that the good news is sustained.

Some of the revisions naturally lend themselves to advancing the conversation in a particular way. For example, you may have noticed that the Apply revision often includes the sense of 'qualifying' the OP or her company in some way:

> "The fact that you do *not* have [situation or problem X] means you are precisely the sort of client/company we can help the most."

3. Software Deadline

A freelance software project manager talking to a prospective client in a large company.

"I know you're under a lot of pressure because you need fairly quick turnaround on phase 1 deliverables of about 4-6 weeks?"

"Er, no, I think the plan is 3 - 4 months."

"Right, that's what I mean, fairly short-term. The point is you don't want this to be one of those projects that drag on for years and never seem to get anywhere."

4. Party Singer

A singer talking to a prospect organising a large party.

"It's never easy organising something like this, is it? It's a largely thankless task and you're worried about how to keep guests entertained when they arrive, and during dinner, plus how do you keep the kids occupied, and then there's the after-dinner part of the evening..."

"I'm mostly worried about what to do as guests arrive."

"Exactly, you don't want people turning up and getting bored, do you? When your guests arrive I can already be singing a few songs based on your preferences, just to add a bit of background and get people in the right mood..."

5. Events Organiser

An events organiser liaising with the producer of a large trade conference.

"I expect it feels a bit daunting, doesn't it, with all the things you need to take care of? Venue, staging, sound and lights, catering, entertainment and so on..."

"We're not sure how to get staging set up in the gallery."

"That's one of the main reasons I wanted to talk to you. Staging can be a real headache but we have a subsidiary company that specialises in precisely that."

6. Management Consultant

A management consultant meeting with a prospect from a big retail conglomerate.

"Your group is thinking of bringing more of your manufacturing in-house, so there's less reliance on outsourcing, right?"

"Er, not really. We think the current arrangements work pretty well."

"Oh, well, that's good. I mentioned it because, as you know, many companies in your sector *are* cutting back on outsourcing. The fact that you're not suggests you've got your supply chain working pretty well — which is precisely why we should be talking."

7. Marketing Matters

A marketing agency representative to the manager of a plastics company.

"I expect you've been discussing the marketing of the new vinyl coating — the online launch, getting samples out, trade press, targeted ads and so on."

"Well, no, for me it's all about getting the product right."

"Oh sure, that has to be your priority as you're heading up the project. Other people can worry all about the small details of the launch and so on. But getting the product right is where we can help you, with phased roll-out, split tests, customer surveys, online assessment tools and so on."

8. Training Company

The manager of a training company visiting a bank's HR manager.

"I know one of your challenges, that you've probably had a lot of meetings about, is putting together a team to handle the new rules on accounts transfer."

"Actually, no, that's not a major focus for us."

"Well, not at the moment, no. But it is something you'll need to address over the next 18 months so I felt we should have a chat about it now."

Section 2: Communication Skills

"Laughter is a release of tension. When influencing, make the other person laugh; you'll gain rapport instantly."

— Marshall Sylver

1. The Ten Second Smile

CRFB is essentially a communication skill. It's a way of achieving all the things I listed under the Tarot Comparison right at the start of this book. In this section, I want to share additional communication skills that I believe are worth knowing. They can make a tremendous difference to every aspect of your life.

In my opinion, the ten second smile is the single greatest communication skill you can learn. With this skill, you are well on your way to being a communication expert. Without it, I doubt you can be.

The ten second smile consists of a simple challenge. Whenever you meet someone for the first time, aim to get a smile or a small laugh out of them within ten seconds. This is not about learning to be a clown or a stand-up comedian. It's about saying something that demonstrates your *interest*, *observation* and *empathy*. It's also about harnessing the wonderful power of humour to connect, build bridges and put people at their ease.

As with any skill, it's a smart idea to practise when it *doesn't* matter so you'll be good when it *does*. It's particularly easy to practise the ten second smile. Every day of your life, you can practise on all the wonderful people who work in the service industries: shopkeepers, assistants, receptionists, waiters, cleaners, guides, door staff, drivers and so on. These people deserve your gratitude, love and respect. Make it your business to cause them to smile and try to get there within ten seconds. This is not just a great communication skill to learn. It's also a nice thing to do and, in a small way, helps to make the world a nicer, warmer and friendlier place. Unfortunately, people in the service industries are often treated very badly, as if they are some sort of inferior species.

I was once at a train station and stopped by a small stand selling tea and coffee. I never touch coffee but I do drink heroic quantities of tea. There was a young assistant behind the counter, all on her own. This was about 4 pm in the afternoon and the stand was fairly quiet. I got my tea, went into ten second smile mode and enjoyed a short, pleasant chat with the assistant.

"It makes a nice change," said the assistant. "You're the first person who's actually talked to me all day." She explained that normally she only had purely functional exchanges with customers: they said what they wanted, she handed it over, they paid and left. At very busy times, I do understand that people tend to have these purely functional conversations. The sad thing is that even at much quieter times, when there's no rush and customers *could* treat the Service Industry Army with kindness and recognition, they rarely do so.

2. Before You Talk

Strange as it may seem, there are some good communication skills you can use *before* you even say a word! Here are a few good ideas you may like to try.

Welcome Energy

Nicholas Boothman wrote a fascinating book called, 'How To Make People Like You In 90 Seconds Or Less'. One of his suggestions is that, when you meet someone for the first time, you imagine that you're sending something like a ball of light, warmth and energy out from yourself and towards them.

I stress that this is a purely *imaginary* activity and no-one else needs to even be aware that you're doing it. While it may sound like a rather strange thing to do, if you try it I think you'll find it's actually a remarkably good idea. If nothing else, it *reminds* you to adopt a welcoming disposition and to *look* and *sound* as if you're actually pleased to see the other person. The 'ball of energy' may not be real, but the effects of imagining it travelling from you to the other person most certainly are.

Mind Scripts

Mind scripts are a simple yet powerful idea that anyone can use to improve how well they communicate. A mind script consists of three short, simple statements about:

- You.

- The OP.

- The situation and desired outcome.

You can devise a mind script to suit almost any meeting you are going to be involved in. For example, here's one you might devise if you're going for a job interview:

- I'm a really great candidate.

- This is a really great company.

- I expect this will go really well.

Here's another one that you might use before a sales pitch:

- I've got a really great product.

- S/he is a really likeable client.

- S/he will love this and we'll agree a deal.

You get the idea. So, what's the point of a mind script and why is it useful?

We all communicate with one another in many ways all the time. There's a lot more to communication than just the words you use. There's also *how* you say them: emphasis, intonation, inflection and so on. In addition, there are all the elements of non-verbal communication (NVC), such as your facial expression, gestures and body language.

In order to communicate effectively, all these different aspects of the way you communicate have to *cohere*. They have to all convey the same message. If you are using very enthusiastic *words* but your *tone* suggests doubt, you won't communicate very well. Likewise if your *emphasis* is bright and positive but your *facial expression* suggests boredom.

The problem is that it's hard to *consciously* align all these elements. It is sometimes jokingly suggested that if a centipede tried to *consciously* control all its legs, it wouldn't be able to. The task is just too complex. It's the same with all these different aspects of how you communicate. It's difficult to *consciously* orchestrate your words, tone and non-verbal communication so they all convey the same message.

A mind script enables you to do this. By preparing a mind script and using it, you can get all the various aspects of how you communicate to cohere. Just running the three simple statements through your mind makes all the difference.

How do you use a mind script? First of all, it's *not* something you ever say out loud, at least not when anyone else is listening! Just prepare your mind script and then rinse it through your mind five or ten minutes before your meeting. Do the same again once or twice just before the meeting. That's all there is to it!

Interestingly, you can also use your mind script *during* a meeting. You might think that if you were talking to someone, and ran your mind script through your head during the conversation, this would lead to a mental crashing of gears. However, most people find there's no problem at all. A mind script is so short and simple that you can sustain a conversation perfectly well even if you flash your mind script through your head once or twice. Try it!

Be Special

Imagine you go to a business conference and chat to a few different people. Afterwards, you talk about the experience to your partner or a work colleague. Which of the following scenarios sounds more appealing to you?

You could say, "It was okay, nothing special. Met a few people. Talked about the project. The usual stuff."

Or you could say, "I met the most *extraordinary* person! She was *amazing*! She had some *fantastic* ideas that I really think could make a big difference to the project. And she's been all over the world and knows all these *brilliant* contacts, including some people who might be *seriously* interested in buying the system once it's finished! We need to get the team together for a meeting with her as soon as possible!"

The fact is, people enjoy meeting someone special. It's interesting, exciting and thought-provoking, and can often stimulate fresh ideas or new ways of thinking. It brightens their day and puts a smile on their face. There's enough that's boring and familiar in the world. Having a 'special' experience makes a nice change.

This being the case, *don't be afraid to be someone special.* Give people that pleasure, that spark of delight that brightens their day and stimulates some fresh thoughts and new ideas. It's a nice thing to do.

Whenever I mention this point, I find myself having to hack through a dense thicket of misinterpretations. I'm not saying you have to be loud, conceited or egocentric. You can be quiet and modest yet still be someone special. Nor am I saying you should have an exaggerated sense of your own importance or believe yourself to be perfect. You can accept yourself as a simple, flawed human being, and yet still be someone special for people to meet.

More specifically, be aware of your *value*, the help you can offer and the difference you can make to someone's life. Sometimes, one encouraging comment is all it takes.

A long time ago, I was contemplating leaving my job and working for myself. I felt unsure about taking what seemed, at the time, to be quite a momentous step. One evening, I was having an informal chat with a friend over a drink. We talked about all sorts of things and only briefly touched on my thoughts about working for myself. My friend, in a very matter-of-fact way, shrugged and said, "Oh, I think you'd probably be all right. There are plenty of people working for themselves who aren't as good as you."

That was all she said. She wasn't even trying to be nice or to say something encouraging. It was just a simple, honest opinion woven into the flow of the conversation. However, her comment resonated with me and played its part in my decision to quit my job.

Give people the pleasure of meeting someone special. Don't underestimate your ability to make a difference, even if it's just by taking an interest, being positive and offering encouragement. Whenever you're going to meet new people, decide in advance that you'll be the 'someone special' they mention enthusiastically afterwards.

Being special doesn't mean going on an ego trip. Think of it as being distinctive, believing in yourself *and* the people you meet equally, making your contribution and helping people all you can.

Benign Expertise

Not many things are universally loved, but benign expertise is one of them. Like pizza, kittens and 'Catch 22', it is always liked, always welcomed, never rejected.

You can't get your computer to print something. You have wrestled with it, tried everything you know, checked everything and even switched it off and on again... yet the recalcitrant and downright malevolent computer refuses to print, cackling with contempt at your feeble yet desperate attempts to force its cooperation. It smirks at your helplessness and sits in happy, mute defiance of your screamed invective.

The expert comes along. She assesses the situation, nods to herself and mutters something about an overflow stack error. She taps a command or clicks a mouse and, as if by supreme magical power, the computer does what you want it to do.

You can't get your car to start. You try everything, go through every rite and ritual you can think of that might possibly persuade the car to roar into life and actually transport you from A to B — the one, single task it was created and designed to perform. No joy, no luck, no mechanical stirrings of readiness to serve. It's a cold, wet day. Time is passing and you fear you will never get to that Very Important Place to do that Very Important Thing. Your car remains smug, silent and static, its sleek metallic skin conveying its shiny disdain for your pathetic efforts to secure its compliance.

The expert comes along. She listens to what happens when you try the ignition, casts an eye over the engine and mumbles something about a loose blade fuse. She loosens a panel you didn't even know existed, fiddles with something, snaps the panel back into place and invites you to try once more. The car immediately roars into life and humbly begs to be your eager servant, your preferred mode of conveyance to anywhere, anywhere at all.

We all love a benign expert: someone who not only has expertise but who is happy to place that expertise at *your* disposal to make *your* problem go away.

When you want to communicate successfully, see if you can play the role of the benign expert. Of course, this won't be possible in every situation. However, keep an eye out for those occasions when it *is* possible. Also, keep an open mind about the notion of 'expertise'. Something that you find easy might seem like the work of a genius to someone else. I once tuned a guitar for a friend, something I regard as a trivially easy to do. He looked at me with the kind of awe normally reserved for movie stars and deities.

In my capacity as a freelance writer, I once turned up at a company and looked at their list of things they needed me to write. Trust me when I say it was all very routine stuff — just bits and pieces of their corporate communications that any tech writer could happily wrangle into shape. I gave a relaxed shrug and said I'd be able to get it done in a couple of weeks (and that some of it could be automated anyway). I wasn't trying to impress anyone.

My contact at the company stared at me with open-mouthed disbelief. "We've been trying to get all this done for about six months! And we figured you'd need at least three."

I once knew a salesman for a company that sold video cameras and related equipment. He never referred to himself as a salesman. Instead, he played the role of a benign expert. He used to call production companies and say, "Look, in your business, you need to know what equipment's on the market, what the latest kit can do and what works best. I will come along, talk about all the latest gear and what it does and then go away. As and when you actually want to buy some new stuff, maybe you'll give me a call, maybe not. Either way, at least you'll have good information from an expert."

He made a *lot* of sales.

Where possible, be a source of benign expertise. You will make a lot of friends, create a lot of smiles and communicate *very* successfully with people.

3. How You Talk

So far, we've looked at the ten second smile and some communication skills you can use *before* you even say a word. Now let's look at skills you can use once you actually start talking.

Flowing Delivery

When you're using CRFB, a smooth, flowing delivery is immensely beneficial. The same goes for any successful spoken communication.

Every hesitation, every instance of 'um' and 'er', damages the communication process. It's not hard to see why. 'Um' and 'er' and similar sounds don't convey any information. In technical terms, they are 'noise' rather than 'signal'. Anyone listening to you has to filter them out in order to concentrate on what you're actually saying.

Which of the next two paragraphs do you find easier, and more pleasant, to read?

> 'Your clients blank usually phone er to [noise] discuss um things before er deciding blank whether to um actually go ahead and, sorry, hold on, make a booking. Imagine um you handle most blank of these [noise] calls. What noise sort of triplets could um you use?'

> 'Your clients usually phone to discuss things before deciding whether to actually go ahead and make a booking. Imagine you handle most of these calls. What sort of triplets could you use?'

Of course, achieving a smooth, flowing delivery without too many glitches is easier said than done. You can't achieve flawless eloquence just by wishing for it.

I can offer two slivers of advice, one obvious and the other not *quite* so obvious. The obvious point is that, as with everything else, practice and experience are the best teachers and the only ones you can really rely on. There's no substitute for experience, for learning by doing. As the proverb says, 'The difference between a master and a beginner is that the master has failed more often than the beginner has even tried.'

The second and marginally less obvious bit of advice is what I'll call the guitarist's secret. I've spent about 35 years learning to play the guitar not very well. I own a truly beautiful Maldonado classical guitar. She's my pride and joy and, in truth, she deserves to be owned by someone who could get better music out of her. Here's the point: how do guitarists learn

Good sales professionals know about Carnegie's worm principle even if they call it something else. When you're selling, don't talk about the product features *you* find interesting. Ask the customer what he or she is interested in and focus on that. There's no point raving about how fast a car can go if the customer's main concern is safety and how economical it is to run.

Don't talk about what *you* happen to know about. Don't talk about what *you* find interesting. Talk about what *your audience* will find interesting and what *they* want to learn from you.

The Sweetest Sound

I'm going to quote from Dale Carnegie again. He said, "A person's name is to that person the sweetest and most important sound in any language."

It you want to communicate successfully, remember to use the name of the person you're talking to from time to time. It's their favourite sound and the one that will *always* get their attention. This is just the way people are wired up.

By extension, 'you' is everyone's favourite pronoun. If you and I are having a conversation, and I talk about myself all the time, you'll hear a lot of 'I' and 'my' sounds. These sounds aren't very exciting for your brain. From your point of view, the conversation would seem a lot more interesting if you were hearing 'you' and 'your' sounds instead. These sounds would also make your brain light up more.

What's interesting is that you can change the pronouns and still say more or less the same things. You just have to be a little creative. "I've had this great idea" becomes "You might like this idea". "I've got a great story" becomes "Listen, you might like this story." "I've been working a lot on this problem" becomes "You asked me to look at this problem and you might like one of the solutions I've found."

I'm not saying it's *always* good to robotically avoid the first person pronoun and twist *every* sentence into a 'you' shape. Stiff rules don't make for natural, pleasant conversation. The point is to recognise that 'you' has a lot of currency. It means your communication isn't entirely self-focused, that you're trying to engage with the other person and inviting their participation.

Yes / Free / Now

People listen to the radio station that most often plays the kind of music they enjoy listening to. When you want to communicate successfully with people, it's worth remembering three sounds everyone loves: 'yes', 'free' and 'now'.

Yes

'Yes' is everyone's favourite answer.

Life is full of disappointing and frustrating answers: no, can't, never, not yet, not open, not available, not possible. The world offers a limitless abundance of such answers and never stops making more. It's what I call a 'cacophany of not-ness' and it can be quite frustrating. This is why it can seem so refreshing to hear the opposite sounds: 'yes' and 'can'.

One of the reasons we all meet 'no' more often than 'yes' is that 'no' is *always* the easier and more convenient answer. Once I've told you I can't or won't do something, that's the end of the story. When I tell you I can or I will, I have to actually take some action or make something happen. We all know this, which is another reason why 'yes' so often has a warm glow attached to it. You enjoy thinking someone is actually going to make an effort and do something for you (assuming they are reliable and do, in fact, follow through.)

This feeling is amplified when there is some problem-solving involved. "No, I can't do that because the office has closed," is one answer, and will never bring joy into the world.

Here's a different type of answer: "That wouldn't normally be possible because the office has closed. But there's got to be a way to do this. Let me think about it and see what I can come up with for you." This cannot ever *fail* to bring joy into the world.

Free

'Free' is everyone's favourite price.

This is not a point wasted on the advertising industry, which makes sure the world is drenched with free offers, free quotes, free estimates, free trial periods, free introductory sessions and free gifts (such as the massively generous free pen, worth 50p, that comes with the holiday home rental agreement or the expensive insurance policy). There are so many free offers it's surprising anyone pays for anything at all.

The psychology of 'free' is fascinating. We are all perfectly well aware that 'free' is often a treacherous two-faced trickster, a wolf in sheep's advertising. This isn't because we're all jaded, cynical souls unable to appreciate the joy of the sunrise and the grandeur of the stars. It's because we've all seen the trick exposed so often that we know 'free' is, at best, 'free-ish' and often 'actually quite expensive'. We've seen the man behind the curtain so we don't fall for the 'Oz' routine as readily as we once did.

At least, that's what you'd think. The fact is, even though we all know that 'free' is usually fake, it still works and is very hard to compete with. There is still a part of your brain, and mine, that can't help being interested in the magical possibility that maybe, just maybe, there's an opportunity to get something for nothing.

Now

'Now' is everyone's favourite timescale.

Ann can process your order next week. Ben can do it the day after tomorrow and Ken can do it now. All else being equal, the world is going to choose Ken.

Prompt service has always been popular, but the expectation of instant gratification is a trend that's only going in one direction. We live in the age of magic technology, all of which encourages impatient attitudes. No technology ever became popular because it made things take longer to do. I'm old enough to remember writing letters to friends in America. My letter took ten days to arrive and theirs, assuming an instant response, took ten days to get back to me. Now people feel aggrieved if they send someone a text message and don't get a reply within five minutes.

Using 'Yes, Free, Now'

Given that people like the words 'yes' 'free' and 'now' more than they like the alternatives, try to include them in your business communications as often as possible (within reason).

Whenever you talk to people about possibilities, price or timescale, try to include 'yes free now' as far as you can. Give the person you're talking to the delight, the joy of hearing these three magical, seductive words.

At this point, you may want to raise a common objection: you understand the *theory* behind 'yes free now', but it's not often *practical* to use these words in real life. You can't always say yes to customers, your goods aren't free and you can't supply them immediately.

I accept that opportunities to use these words in your business communications are not always *naturally occurring*. However, you can *create* opportunities to use them.

Here's a simple example from real life. I once did a bit of consultancy work for a graphic design company. They were definitely not always in a position to say 'yes' to potential customers who called. Also, their work was never free nor was it possible to deliver 'now' — even 'rush' jobs tended to take a day or two.

I suggested they created a simple sales brochure containing answers to common questions and information about some of the 'standard' packages they offered such as corporate ID design, business cards and stationery. I helped them to create this as a pdf file they could send instantly by email to anyone who called.

When they received phone enquiries, they could often say something like this:

> "**Yes**, we can do that for you or something very similar. And I can send you our **free** guide that gives you most of the information you want, and I can send it to you right **now**. What's your email address?"

This meant the majority of their callers were hearing the sounds 'yes', 'free' and 'now'. They told me this made a significant difference to the number of calls that they converted into profitable work. Even when you don't think you can use these golden, attractive sounds in your communication, you probably can if you think about it. And you should.

Sometimes, you can use 'yes, free, now' in a very simple way. I was told about a builder who often got calls from people hoping he'd be able to do some work for them quite quickly. He noticed something. If he said, "No, sorry, I can't help. I wouldn't be able to come over until later this week," he tended to lose the job. If he said, "Yes, I can help. In fact I can come round soon, probably later this week," he tended to get the job. Same situation, different words.

If you want people to like your radio station, play their favourite sounds: yes, free, now.

5. Building Rapport

The dictionary says that 'to build rapport' means 'to foster a relationship of trust and agreement'. I like to think of it as human resonance. If you put two violins at opposite ends of a room and pluck the 'A' string on one of them, the same string on the other violin will start to vibrate. People can resonate with one another in a similar way.

Invest In Interest

Everyone has their story. When you meet people, take a *genuine* interest in them. Ask questions and give them the pleasure of talking about themselves, who they are and how they came to *be* who they are. This is your fast path to rapport: listen and appreciate.

Here's an interesting way to look at it. Imagine dozens of newborn babies in the maternity wing of a hospital. At just a few days old, the babies are basically all alike. They sleep, cry, get fed and changed. That's it.

Imagine those babies thirty years later. Some will be intellectual, others will barely have read a book. Some will be hale and hearty outdoor types, others will be couch potatoes who prefer to be indoors, dry and warm. Some will care next to nothing for politics, others will have strong and possibly extreme views. Some will love jazz, others rock or classical. There will be sociable types and loners, hellraisers and wallflowers, high achievers and aimless drifters.

In each and every case, it's fascinating to think how this person came to be who they are. Think of all the nurture and nature factors, plus choices and decisions, involved in the path from 'babe in a cot' to you, me and everyone else — all different and all with a story to tell.

If you make it your business to listen to everyone, you will enjoy wonderful stories. Among many others, I remember the Greek taxi driver in Vegas whose family smuggled gold out of Germany in the war; the refugee who started with nothing and ended up running a power company; the psychologist who prided himself on being Leonard Cohen's number one fan; and the railway engineer who wrote plays and song lyrics in his spare time.

One final tip: try to listen without *judgment*. If you're judging, you're not listening. Try not to get distracted by whether you agree or disagree with the other person's views and preferences. Listen, learn and enjoy the privilege of exploring another person's life and testimony. Every story is a free lesson in human nature, and a lesson worth knowing.

The Thurber Principle

James Thurber was a wonderfully gifted writer and cartoonist. If you're not familiar with his work, I strongly recommend that you give yourself a treat and take a look at it. I doubt you'll be disappointed.

Thurber came up with one of the finest, most brilliant definitions I've ever read. He defined humour as 'emotional turbulence recalled in tranquillity'. Isn't that just beautiful?

To see the relevance to successful communication, imagine two friends having a conversation. One shares a funny story about, say, getting hopelessly lost somewhere. Her friend says, "I know just what you mean! Something similar happened to me when..." and tells her story. People enjoy sharing stories and discovering that they have been through similar experiences.

You can use this idea when you're trying to communicate successfully with people. Look for any types of 'emotional turbulence' that you have both been through in the past. Think of similar problems you have both probably faced, or similar frustrations that, while annoying at the time, you can joke about in retrospect.

Many comedians specialise in 'observational' comedy, highlighting everyday problems and annoyances that their audience can relate to. You don't have to be a comedian to use this technique. In business meetings, you can often introduce a point by saying, "I'm sure, like me, you've often experienced a situation where..." and then describe a problem everyone can identify with.

We tend to bond with people whom we feel have been through similar problems. Looking back on those problems, and having a laugh about them, feels very cathartic. This is the Thurber principle. Use it to your advantage as often as possible.

One short additional note: I dabble in the world of magic and mindreading. When magicians and other entertainers hang out, which is always enjoyable, we rarely talk about *successful* shows and the times when everything went well. Those tales may be good for the ego but they aren't a lot of fun. We much prefer to share tales of 'disaster' gigs and 'shows from hell' where everything that could go wrong did so in spectacular fashion. This is another manifestation of the Thurber principle.

Emperor / Slave

Here's one more rapport tip that I think you'll enjoy. When you meet someone for the first time, ask yourself a question: *how does this person expect to be received?*

Some people go through life behaving like an Emperor. When they enter a room, they give the impression that they *expect* to treated deferentially, to have authority and to tell people what to do rather than be told. They expect to enjoy certain privileges (the best seat, the best view) and to have small tasks performed for them (such as someone bringing them coffee).

Other people convey a quite different impression, almost as if they have a Slave mentality. When they enter a room, they seem devoid of authority and look like they're just waiting to be told what to do — and that they will readily comply. They don't expect any privileges and expect to have to do everything for themselves.

I'm painting in very broad brushstrokes here, and there are many more possibilities than just these two extreme examples. As well as Emperors and Slaves, there are Performers and Watchers, Leaders and Followers, Givers and Takers and many more options besides. Just give yourself a moment to look at the person, assess how they expect to be received and form a few conclusions about them. This is speculative, of course, and you won't always be 100% correct, but it's worth doing anyway. Let me put it this way: doing this is at least more informative than *not* doing it.

If you want to build good rapport with that person, conform to their expectations as far as you can. When you are part of the experience they *expect* to have, they feel comfortable with you and the channels of communication will be open. If you behave otherwise, you become an uncomfortable presence, a piece that doesn't fit in the jigsaw. These feelings do not promote good rapport.

IBIY

There is a wonderful gift that you can give to people. It cost nothing, takes a second, yet it can mean a lot and make a *huge* difference. In fact, it can actually change someone's life in a very positive way.

Just say, "I believe in you", or words to that effect.

There are many people with an impressive track record of success. Most will tell you that when they were just starting out, they were helped and encouraged by the one or two people who said, "I believe in you".

There are many people who could have achieved great things, but they never tried because there was no-one there to say, "I believe in you". They could have given us great inventions, started successful companies, written brilliant music, solved important problems, completed important books, created an empire… but they didn't, because nobody ever said, "I believe in you".

Very often, the only thing people need in order to start on their path to success is someone to express a little faith in them, to offer some encouragement. There are always plenty of voices saying the opposite. Whatever you try to achieve in life, there will always be people doubting you and making it clear they don't think much of your potential. Offering someone a simple "I believe in you" can make a big difference.

You don't have to do this in a loud or conspicuous way. It can be enough just to be chatting to someone and say, "I reckon you'd probably be able to do that," or, "Sounds like a pretty good plan to me,"or, "I think your work has a lot of potential".

However you say it, whatever words you choose, saying "I believe in you" can make a profound difference to someone's life.

Why am I mentioning this here? Because one of the greatest, fastest ways to build rapport with anyone is just to say words that convey this simple idea: "I believe in you".

This only works if you're sincere. You don't necessarily need to believe in *every* aspect of *every* plan or dream someone mentions. But you can usually focus on at least one aspect of a dream or a goal and find a way to say, "I believe in you". It creates wonderful rapport.

And makes the world a much better place.

6. Hypnotic Language

Just to be clear, I neither practise nor teach hypnosis. If you want to learn about this fascinating subject, I suggest you contact the two finest exponents I know: Anthony Jacquin and Igor Ledochowsky. They're both experts, great to work with and good company.

When I refer to 'hypnotic' language, I just mean a few ways to become a more interesting and compelling speaker. In this book, I want to focus on two in particular.

Hook Lines

A hook line is a deliberately *incomplete* thought that more or less forces the listener to want to hear more. For example:

"There's one remarkable difference between us and every other company in our industry. Yet hardly anyone realises it."

If you heard someone say this, you would feel more or less compelled to keep listening until you found out what this 'remarkable difference' was. Here's another example:

"I've gone over the proposal carefully. You know something? There's one detail we've all overlooked and yet it could make a huge difference."

Again, you feel compelled to listen until you know what this detail is. Good hook lines often include the notion of opposites:

"We're a tech company, but what we need right now actually has nothing at all to do with technology".

"I was looking at our sales figures and I realised there's one trick we're missing. And it's nothing to do with the way we actually sell."

Hook lines are a brilliant way to start a conversation, meeting, sales pitch, negotiation, speech or presentation. They tap into our natural sense of intrigue and our instinctive need for semantic resolution, for closure and for statements *not* to leave us 'waiting for the other shoe to drop'.

This is my favourite 'hypnotic' language technique of all. It works so well that it's *almost* unfair. I love thinking of hook lines and putting them to good use.

The Power Of Stories

It's an excellent idea to express ideas in stories. They are often the best and most memorable way to get a point across. Most great teachers, preachers and leaders use stories and the power of narrative to get their point across. Throughout history, people have coded important messages in fables, myths, jokes, tales and legends. People *like* stories and good ones tend to endure and get passed around. Hence if you want to communicate successfully, see if you can present what you want to say in the form of a story, allegory or metaphor.

I would advise you *not* to just scrape stories off the internet. It's certainly *possible* to do this: there are websites full of anecdotes and parables that executives can stuff into speeches to illustrate one theme or another. However, it's *not* a good idea to do this — not unless you want to advertise your laziness and tragic lack of originality and imagination. What's more, when you tell the story you won't sound authentic.

It's a much better idea, wherever possible, to use a story drawn from your experience. You'll be authentic and original, and you'll also sound much better than you would if you were merely reciting something you got from a website.

One of the themes I sometimes mention in my work is the importance of seeing possibilities that other people miss. Whenever I need to illustrate this point, I tell my Madame Tussauds story. It's from real life, it conveys the point in a delightful way and it's *my* story: no-one else has it and no-one I'm talking to will have heard it before. I think this is better than rehashing an old, anonymous anecdote grabbed from a website ten minutes before the meeting.

Use Agreement

Wherever possible and appropriate, agree with the OP (other person or other party).

It is often the case that, when someone asks you a question, you know their own opinion on the matter. Wherever possible, offer agreement rather than disagreement. Of course, you can devise obvious counter-examples. If you're talking to someone with deluded, dangerous, fanatical views, agreeing isn't a great idea. However, unless you're having some very strange business meetings these days, and your career has taken an unfortunate turn, I doubt you will often be in this position.

Bear in mind that you don't have to offer 100% agreement. There are many shades of grey in between total agreement and the opposite. It's perfectly all right to say things like, "I think I'm broadly in agreement with you," and, "We might differ on a few details but overall I think we're on the same page."

TTWTWTH

This stands for 'Tell them what they want to hear'. When you're using Fallback Answers, do this often as possible.

On some occasions you might not *know* what the OP wants to hear. However, this is quite rare. Most of the time, you will either know the answer people want you to give or you can deduce it from the way they ask the question, their intonation, phrasing, body language and so on. It's relatively rare for people to ask questions in a totally neutral way that signals nothing about their own preferences.

Use Safe Sources

It's often good to mention relevant sources in a Fallback Answer. There are many sources worth mentioning, including both popular and specialist media. For example, if you're answering a question about business and the economy, you could refer to a magazine, or news and current affairs show, that is seen as having some authority and weight (in your country). Alternatively, if you know of a specialist publication, site, bulletin or podcast that is regarded as authoritative, you might want to refer to it in your answer.

However, it's important to only mention *safe* sources. A safe source is simply *one that can never be checked*. A good way to turn a source into a safe source is to never mention a date. For example, I live in the UK where there is a weekly magazine called 'The Economist'. As the name suggests, it's primarily full of articles about economic news and current affairs. I could say something like this:

> "That's an interesting point and, in fact, I read in The Economist just last week that manufacturing is actually growing much faster than expected..."

This isn't a safe source because it can be checked. It's possible for someone to demonstrate, or know, that you're wrong. You might be talking to someone who has read last week's edition and knows perfectly well that there was no such article or you haven't understood it correctly. Here's a much better version:

> "That's an interesting point and, in fact, I think I read in The Economist recently that manufacturing is actually growing much faster than expected..."

This is safe because no-one can ever demonstrate, or know, that you are incorrect. 'Recently' could mean at any point over the past few months, and in any case you only said you *think* it was in The Economist. It might have been another publication that deals with the same subject matter.

Predict The Future

Fallback Answers are often useful when it comes to talking about future events. You may feel that you lack the ability to forecast the future and, unlike Nostradamus, were not born with the gift of powerful, accurate prophecy. Let me give you some good news. You can, in fact, foretell the future. What's more, you can do so with exceptional accuracy.

Forget about vague guesses or bland statements that could mean almost anything. You have the power to make specific, faultless predictions. You can read the future as easily as you're reading these words. Do you doubt me? Well, doubt no more. I shall bestow this power upon you right now.

The first principle you need to know about is 'fog now, clarity later'. This simply means that the picture will be clearer in the future than it is now. You may think this sounds as dull as it is obvious, and you're right. It is. However, you can make it *sound* like profound insight. Consider, for example, the precious metals market. Is it heading up or down? Here's the answer:

> "Well, I'm sure you're as aware as I am that there are probably as many views on this question as there are people to offer them! Clearly, there have been some mixed signals over the last couple

of market cycles. Right now, I'd say there's good news in the sense that we're definitely entering a phase where some of the volatility is going to disappear. We'll see the market enter a more settled phase and I think if you look say, three to four months out, stronger trends will emerge making it much easier for investors to choose a direction."

That's 'fog now, clarity later' in 100 words. Using the same basic formula, you can now confidently predict wheat prices in Asia over the next six months or the price of semiconductors in Europe next year.

Another way to peer into the future with impressive accuracy is to always predict 'regression to the mean'. If you know a bit about statistics, you will already understand this term. If not, here's a simplified explanation. Consider any value you can track over a period of time, such as the price of a ton of wheat. If you follow the price over a given period, you can calculate the *average* value. The further the current value is from the historical average, the more likely it is to move *towards* that average.

If the price is now *slightly* higher or lower than the average value, it is *slightly* likely to start moving back towards that average. If the price is *very* different from the average value, we can be *very* confident it will soon head back towards the average.

As with 'fog now, clarity later', there is no need to use a few words when many will do. It's not hard to make your words sound suspiciously like shrewd analysis. What's going to happen to the demand for steel in South America over the next year? You know the answer:

"Well, the demand for steel is always like a ship in strong winds, isn't it? It gets pushed this way and that by any number of factors. Medium- to long-term trends in the manufacturing sector are obviously one key factor but there are many others, including shifts in mining costs plus the fact that you have both public and private sector suppliers. But my research suggests we'll see strong movement towards what have been historical levels of demand, with the velocity largely proportional to the deviation from tracked historical data."

That's the 90 word version of 'regression to the mean'.

At this point, my more sceptical readers might dismiss these examples, saying no sane person would ever say such things or accept them as intelligent answers. I might have agreed with you if not for the fact that I spent about ten months of my life working for a financial forecasting company. The Managing Director was a former Big Kahuna from the London Stock Exchange who could talk about currency markets all day and often did. The company produced weekly and monthly reports about a range of dazzlingly exciting subjects, such as the long-term value of the Faroese krona against the Mauritian rupee. It was, let me assure you, every bit as fascinating as it sounds.

Being merely 'the writer guy', I took my rightful place at the bottom of the company's power structure. Every day I was surrounded by a team of economists and analysts speaking in tongues. They produced the numbers and I turned them into readable reports.

I once asked an awkward question at a staff meeting. "If we actually know which way currency markets are going to go, and can predict these movements with a success rate greater than chance, why do we need customers? We could just invest the firm's capital every day and enjoy easy profits." I was told this question was unwelcome and impertinent, and that I ought to get on with my work.

So far as I could tell, most of the company's output relied on 'fog now, clarity later' and 'regression to the mean'. The reports we produced were an elaborate exercise in what my tribe, professional writers-for-hire, refer to using the technical term 'word stuffing'. If our clients paid for a 1,000 word report, that's what they got — even if the content amounted to, "We're not really sure". I'm not saying I'm proud of this phase of my professional career. However, it was informative and illuminating.

Putting It All Together

To give a Fallback Answer, always start with the 'No Comp Or Def' phrase, making it clear you're will only offer one or two relevant points. Then cheerfully improvise and use the other techniques I've mentioned as appropriate. You don't have to use *every* technique on *every* occasion.

I can't give examples of complete Fallback Answers in this book because the printed page can't convey tone, emphasis and delivery, all of which play their part. However, it's something I'm happy to demonstrate when I teach CRFB, either one-to-one or in a class. It's also something my students seem to enjoy learning to do.

I'm going to conclude this section by intentionally repeating myself, because experience suggests I have to. Fallback Answers are not about 'bluffing' or pretending to know something you don't. They're about removing a common source of anxiety, namely the worry of being asked a question you don't know the answer to. This, in turn, helps you to go into any meeting in a relaxed, confident state of mind. This is what Fallback Answers are all about.

Identifying Revisions: Answers

1. Office Supplies. *Apply*. The sales person is effectively saying 'Although the problem I mentioned may not apply to you, it does apply to a lot of people in similar situations, which is why I mentioned it.'

2. Graphic Design. *Metaphor*. The designer switches from the literal meaning of 'cost' to using that word in a broader sense to represent all the factors the OP has to think about.

3. Software Deadline. *A blend of Measurement and Metaphor*. The specific measurement '4-6 weeks' becomes converted into just a way of saying 'fairly short-term'.

4. Party Singer. *Focus*. The singer mentioned lots of things the OP might be concerned about. The OP responded positively to just one. The singer carried on as if this one issue was the only thing she mentioned.

5. Events Organiser. *Focus*. Exactly the same as #4.

6. Management Consultant. *Apply*. The consultant is effectively saying, 'If that possibility I mentioned doesn't apply to you, it's nonetheless true for many people in your industry, which is why I mentioned it.'

7. Marketing Matters. *A blend of Aware and Focus*. The rep mentioned several ideas. The OP picked up on one and the rep just talks about that as if it was the only thing he mentioned. In addition, he conveys the idea that the OP is too important to be aware of small details his subordinates can take care of.

8. Training Company. *Time*. Though the statement may not be true now, it will be at some point in the future.

9. Technical Talk. *Metaphor*. The manager shifts from 'new tariffs' being understood literally as something worth discussing in its own right to this just being an example of the *type* of thing they may want to discuss.

10. Marketing Bicycles. *Subjective*. The consultant suggests something is good news. The manager says actually, it isn't. The consultant says it is if you look at it a different way.

Love And Gratitude

A lot of people contributed to this book, whether they realise it or not. I'd like to express my thanks and enduring gratitude to all of them.

David Britland was the first person to tell me about cold reading, a long time ago when we were both teenagers fascinated by magic and mentalism. Richard Webster has written more brilliant books on the subject than anyone else ever has or ever will, and is also a very kind and supportive friend.

Darius Ziatabari was the first person to encourage me to present public classes, all the way back in 2008. He helped me organise the first version of what eventually evolved into the CRFB class. I'd also like to thank everyone who signed up for that very first class. Without their support, I might never have held another class or written this book!

John Morgan helped me to run some early versions of the class and was a dependable friend. He was also a lot of fun to work with.

In recent years, I have relied on the fantastically efficient people at www.findmeaconference.com to find and organise my training venues for me. They do a *superb* job, save me a lot of money and make my life a lot easier. I'd like to thank them all, in particular Jennie and Mary.

AJ Green has provided all manner of technical support and help for many years, as well as proving to be a dependable source of support and a great friend.

Mark Hesketh-Jennings is one of the finest and most talented photographers I know and has come along to several of my classes to take excellent promotional photos.

Laylah Garner is a very talented graphic designer whose wonderful services I've used over many years. She came up with the main design element on the front cover.

Barry Cooper is a brilliant proofreader who dutifully waded through my many, many mistakes and corrected them.

I also want to thank everyone who has ever studied CRFB with me, either one-to-one via the internet, one-to-one in person, or in one of my public classes. It has been a pleasure and a privilege to work with all of you.

Final Words

I love teaching CRFB and I hope you enjoyed learning about it with me. To state the obvious, CRFB is only useful if you actually use it in real life.

Like anything else, using CRFB gets easier with practice and experience. After a while, the 'model' just forms itself in your mind as you go into a particular meeting or discussion. You'll find you can think of subjects, statements and revisions quickly and easily — with barely any effort.

It may take you a while to get there... but it's worth it! Imagine going through the rest of your life with the confidence that you can make a statement about almost anything, to almost anyone, and never actually be wrong! Doesn't that sound great?

If you want to get in touch, by all means send me an email (ian@ianrowland.com or visit any of my websites and use the email link provided). I'd love to hear from you.

May I once again thank all of those who helped to produce this book, and most of all I would like to thank you for reading it.

— Ian Rowland

London, 2020

---

www.ianrowland.com
About my work as a writer-for-hire.

www.coldreadingsuccess.com
Everything to do with cold reading and 'cold reading for business'.

www.ianrowlandtraining.com
My talks and training for conferences, corporate groups and private clients.

End Note 1: An Invitation

Let's Work Together!

Would you like to study CRFB with me? You can!

I provide cold reading tuition both in person and online (via Skype or Zoom). Whether you want to apply CRFB to sales and business situations, or to help you achieve other goals, I'd welcome the opportunity to work with you.

Learning more about the art and practise of cold reading can lead to significant benefits in your personal, social and professional life. It's also great fun! Whatever you'd like to achieve in terms of your CRFB expertise, I can help you get there.

See www.coldreadingsuccess.com for details.

I'd love to work with you!

— Ian Rowland

www.ianrowland.com
www.coldreadingsuccess.com
www.ianrowlandtraining.com

"Ian's special talent lies in his ability to communicate useful information about self-improvement, business, psychology and, yes, magic to diverse audiences around the world. His books are essential reading and if you get the opportunity to hear him speak, don't miss him! For those outside the world of magic and mindreading, let me tell you that Ian is very highly regarded in the trade. He even gets hired to go to major conventions and teach other magicians! When I was Editor of the Magic Circle's magazine, I asked Ian to write a column on mindreading, which he did for 12 years to great acclaim."
— *Matthew Field,* **Member of the Inner Magic Circle**

"I've been an Independent Financial Advisor for 20 years and have learned from people like Dale Carnegie, Anthony Robbins, Jim Rohn and Brian Tracy. I now include Ian Rowland on that list. Having attended his courses and invested in some personal coaching with him, I cannot recommend him highly enough. His unique insights regarding positive persuasion and what makes people tick will prove invaluable in your personal and business life. He's funny, engaging and a leader in his field."
— *Mike LeGassick,* **Leading Independent Financial Advisor**, *UK*

"I make it my business to learn from experts. I spent four days with Ian and we covered a range of skills that I know will help me both personally and professionally — particularly inter-personal skills and ways to establish instant rapport with people. I think he's terrific."
— *Sam Q.,* **Entrepreneur**, *Saudi Arabia*

"I'm a sales guy. I've studied all the big names and been trained by some of the best in the business. I trained with Ian via Skype and he just blew my mind with techniques and perspectives I never knew before. It's all practical. I use what Ian taught me almost every day. He opened my eyes to aspects of communication that truly deserve the term 'magic'."
— *Michael Martin,* **Sales professional**, *USA*

"I studied CRFB with Ian via Skype and without doubt it's my best investment this year! Ian is an excellent teacher and working with him is very enjoyable. In addition, Ian is incredibly generous with his knowledge in many adjacent fields.
— *Patrick Ehrich,* **Teacher and Educational Trainer**, *Germany*

You might like my other books on cold reading.
Available from www.coldreadingsuccess.com in paperback or Kindle.

Printed in Great Britain
by Amazon

80516390R00068